George Washington

The Words of Washington

George Washington

The Words of Washington

ISBN/EAN: 9783744664639

Printed in Europe, USA, Canada, Australia, Japan

Cover: Foto ©ninafisch / pixelio.de

More available books at **www.hansebooks.com**

THE

WORDS OF WASHINGTON.

BEING

Selections from his Most Celebrated State Papers.

———

NEW YORK :

JOHN B. ALDEN, PUBLISHER.

1886.

THE WORDS OF WASHINGTON.

LETTER TO THE GOVERNORS

Newburgh, N. Y., June 18, 1783.

SIR—The object for which I had the honor to hold an appointment in the service of my country being accomplished, I am now preparing to resign it into the hands of Congress, and return to that domestic retirement, which, it is well known, I left with the greatest reluctance; a retirement for which I have never ceased to sigh through a long and painful absence, in which (remote from the noise and trouble of the world), I meditate to pass the remainder of life in a state of undisturbed repose; but, before I carry this resolution into effect, I think it a duty incumbent on me to make this my last official communication, to congratulate you on the glorious events which heaven has been pleased to produce in our favor; to offer my sentiments respecting some important subjects, which appear to me to be intimately connected with the tranquility of the United States; to take my leave of your excellency as a public character; and to give my final blessing to that country, in whose service I have spent the prime of my life; for whose sake I have consumed so many anxious days and watchful nights, and whose happiness, being extremely dear to me, will always constitute no inconsiderable part of my own.

Impressed with the liveliest sensibility on this pleasing occasion, I will claim the indulgence of dilating the more copiously on the subject of our mutual felicitation. When we consider the magnitude of the prize we contended for, the doubtful nature of the contest and the favorable manner in which it has terminated, we shall find the greatest possible reason for gratitude and rejoicing. This is a theme that will afford infinite delight to every benevolent and liberal mind; whether the event in contemplation be considered as a source of present enjoyment, or the parent of future happiness; and we shall have equal occasion to felicitate ourselves on the lot which Providence has assigned us, whether we view it in a natural, a political, or moral point of light.

The citizens of America, placed in the most enviable condition, as the sole lords and proprietors of a vast tract of continent, comprehending all the various soils and climates of the world, and abounding with all the necessaries and conveniences of life, are now, by the late satisfactory pacification, acknowledged to be possessed of absolute freedom and independency; they are from this period to be considered as the actors on a most conspicuous theater, which seems to be peculiarly designed by Providence for the display of human greatness and felicity. Here they are not only surrounded with everything that can contribute to the completion of private and domestic enjoyment, but heaven has crowned all its other blessings, by giving a surer opportunity for political happiness, than any other nation has ever been favored with. Nothing can illustrate these observations more forcibly than a recollection of the happy conjuncture of times and circumstances, under which our republic assumed its rank among the nations. The foundation of our empire was not laid in a gloomy age of ignorance and superstition, but at an epocha when the rights of mankind were better understood and more clearly defined, than at any former period. Researches of the human mind after social happiness have been carried to a great extent; the treasures of knowledge acquired by the labors of philosophers, sages,.and legislators, through a long succession of years are laid open for us, and their collected wisdom may be happily applied in the establishment of our forms of government. The free cultivation of letters, the unbounded extension of commerce, the progressive refinement of manners, the growing liberality of sentiment, and, above all, the pure and benign light of revelation, have had a meliorating influence on mankind, and increased the blessings of society. At this auspicious period, the United States came into existence as a nation; and if their citizens should not be completely free and happy, the fault will be entirely their own.

Such is our situation, and such are our prospects. But notwithstanding the cup of blessing is thus reached out to us; notwithstanding happiness is ours, if we have a disposition to seize the occasion, and make it our own, yet it appears to me there is an

option still left to the United States of America,
whether they will be respectable and prosperous, or
contemptible and miserable as a nation. This is the
time of their political probation: this is the moment
when the eyes of the whole world are turned upon
them; this is the time to establish or ruin their national character forever; this is the favorable moment
to give such a tone to the federal government, as will
enable it to answer the ends of its institution; or,
this may be the ill-fated moment for relaxing the
powers of the union, annihilating the cement of the
confederation, and exposing us to become the sport
of European politics, which may play one state
against another, to prevent their growing importance,
and to serve their own interested purposes. For,
according to the system of policy the states shall
adopt at this moment, they will stand or fall; and
by their confirmation or lapse, it is yet to be decided,
whether the revolution must ultimately be considered
as a blessing or a curse, not to the present age alone,
for with our fate will the destiny of unborn millions
be involved.

With this conviction of the importance of the present crisis, silence in me would be a crime; I will
therefore speak to your excellency the language of
freedom and sincerity, without disguise. I am aware,
however, those who differ from me in political sentiments may, perhaps, remark, I am stepping out of
the proper line of my duty; and they may probably
ascribe to arrogance or ostentation, what I know is
alone the result of the purest intention. But the
rectitude of my own heart, which disdains such un-

worthy motives; the part I have hitherto acted in life; the determination I have formed of not taking any share in public business hereafter, the ardent desire I feel, and shall continue to manifest, of quietly enjoying in private life, after all the toils of war, the benefits of a wise and liberal government, will, I flatter myself, sooner or later, convince my country, that I could have no sinister views in delivering, with so little reserve, the opinion contained in this address.

There are four things which, I humbly conceive, are essential to the well being, I may even venture to say, to the existence, of the United States, as an independent power.

1st. An indissoluble union of the states under one federal head.

2dly. A sacred regard to public justice.

3dly. The adoption of a proper peace establishment. And,

4thly. The prevalence of that pacific and friendly disposition among the people of the United States, which will induce them to forget their local prejudices and policies; to make those mutual concessions, which are requisite to the general prosperity; and in some instances, to sacrifice their individual advantages to the interest of the community.

These are the pillars on which the glorious fabric of our independency and national character must be supported. Liberty is the basis—and whoever would dare to sap the foundation, or overturn the structure, under whatever specious pretext he may attempt it, will merit the bitterest execration, and the severest punishment, which can be inflicted by his injured country.

On the three first articles I will make a few observations, leaving the last to the good sense and serious consideration of those immediately concerned.

Under the first head, although it may not be necessary or proper for me in this place to enter into a particular disquisition of the principles of the union, and to take up the great question which has been frequently agitated, whether it be expedient and requisite for the states to delegate a larger proportion of power to Congress, or not; yet it will be a part of my duty, and that of every true patriot, to assert, without reserve, and to insist upon the following positions:—That, unless the states will suffer Congress to exercise those prerogatives they are undoubtedly invested with by the constitution, everything must very rapidly tend to anarchy and confusion: That it is indispensable to the happiness of the individual states, that there should be lodged, somewhere, a supreme power to regulate and govern the general concerns of the confederated republic, without which the union cannot be of long duration. That there must be a faithful and pointed compliance on the part of every state with the late proposals and demands of Congress, or the most fatal consequences will ensue: That whatever measures have a tendency to dissolve the union, or contribute to violate or lessen the sovereign authority, ought to be considered as hostile to the liberty and independence of America, and the authors of them treated accordingly. And, lastly, that, unless we can be enabled

by the concurrence of the states to participate in the
fruits of the revolution, and enjoy the essential
benefits of civil society, under a form of government
so free and uncorrupted, so happily guarded against
the danger of oppression, as has been devised and
adopted by the articles of confederation, it will be a
subject of regret, that so much blood and treasure
have been lavished for no purpose; that so many
sufferings have been encountered without a compensation, and that so many sacrifices have been made
in vain. Many other considerations might here be
adduced to prove, that, without an entire conformity
to the spirit of the union, we cannot exist as an
independent power. It will be sufficient for my
purpose to mention but one or two, which seem to
me of the greatest importance. It is only in our
united character as an empire, that our independence
is acknowledged, that our power can be regarded, or
our credit supported among foreign nations. The
treaties of the European powers with the United
States of America, will have no validity on a dissolution of the union. We shall be left nearly in a
state of nature; or we may find, by our own unhappy
experience, that there is a natural and necessary
progression from the extreme of anarchy to the
extreme of tyranny; and that arbitrary power is
most easily established on the ruins of liberty, abused
to licentiousness.

As to the second article, which respects the performance of public justice, Congress have, in their
late address to the United States, almost exhausted
the subject; they have explained their ideas so fully,

and have enforced the obligations the states are under to render complete justice to all the public creditors, with so much dignity and energy, that, in my opinion, no real friend to the honor and independency of America can hesitate a single moment respecting the propriety of complying with the just and honorable measures proposed. If their arguments do not produce conviction, I know of nothing that will have greater influence, especially when we reflect that the system referred to, being the result of the collected wisdom of the continent, must be esteemed, if not perfect, certainly the least objectionable, of any that could be devised; and that, if it should not be carried into immediate execution, a national bankruptcy, with all its deplorable consequences, will take place before any different plan can possibly be proposed or adopted; so pressing are the present circumstances, and such is the alternative now offered to the states.

The ability of the country to discharge the debts which have been incurred in its defence, is not to be doubted; and inclination, I flatter myself, will not be wanting. The path of our duty is plain before us; honesty will be found, on every experiment, to be the best and only true policy. Let us then, as a nation, be just; let us fulfill the public contracts which Congress had undoubtedly a right to make for the purpose of carrying on the war, with the same good faith we suppose ourselves bound to perform our private engagements. In the mean time, let an attention to the cheerful performance of their proper business, as individuals, and as members of society, be earnestly inculcated on the citizens of America; then will they strengthen the bands of government, and be happy under its protection. Every one will reap the fruit of his labors; every one will enjoy his own acquisitions, without molestation and without danger.

In this state of absolute freedom and perfect security, who will grudge to yield a very little of his property to support the common interests of society, and ensure the protection of government? Who does not remember the frequent declarations at the commencement of the war—that we should be completely satisfied if, at the expense of one half, we could defend the remainder of our possessions? Where is the man to be found who wishes to remain in debt, for the defence of his own person and property, to the exertions, the bravery, and the blood of others, without making one generous effort to pay the debt of honor and of gratitude? In what part of the continent shall we find any man, or body of men, who would not blush to stand up and propose measures purposely calculated to rob the soldier of his stipend, and the public creditor of his due? And were it possible that such a flagrant instance of injustice could ever happen, would it not excite the general indignation, and tend to bring down upon the authors of such measures the aggravated vengeance of Heaven? If, after all, a spirit of disunion, or a temper of obstinacy and perverseness should manifest itself in any of the states; if such an ungracious disposition should attempt to frustrate all the happy effect that might be expected to flow from the union; if there should be a refusal to comply with requisitions for funds to discharge the annual interest of the public debt; and if that refusal should revive all those jealousies, and produce all those evils, which are now happily removed, Congress, who have in all their transactions shown a great degree of magnanimity and justice, will stand justified in the sight of God and man! and that state alone, which puts itself in opposition to the aggregate wisdom of the continent, and follows such mistaken and pernicious counsels, will be responsible for all the consequences.

For my own part, conscious of having acted, while a servant of the public, in the manner I conceived best suited to promote the real interests of my country; having, in consequence of my fixed belief in some measure pledged myself to the army, that their country would finally do them complete and ample justice, and not wishing to conceal any instance of my official conduct from the eyes of the world, I have thought proper to transmit to your excellency the enclosed collection of papers relative to the half-pay and commutation granted by Congress to the officers of the army. From these communications my decided sentiment will be clearly comprehended, together with the conclusive reasons which induced me, at an early period, to recommend the adoption of this measure in the most earnest and serious manner. As the proceedings of Congress, the army, and myself, are open to all, and contain, in my opinion, sufficient information to remove the prejudices and errors which may have been entertained by any, I think it unnecessary to say anything more than just to observe, that the resolutions of Congress, now alluded to, are as undoubtedly and absolutely binding upon the United States, as the most solemn acts of confederation or legislation.

As to the idea which, I am informed, has in some instances prevailed, that the half-pay and commutation are to be regarded merely in the odious light of a pension, it ought to be exploded forever; that provision should be viewed, as it really was, a reasonable compensation offered by Congress, at a time when they had nothing else to give to officers of the army, for services then to be performed. It was the only means to prevent a total dereliction of the service. It was a part of their hire. I may be allowed to say, it was the price of their blood and of your independency. It is therefore more than a common debt; it is a debt of honor; it can never be considered as a pension, or gratuity, nor canceled until it is fairly discharged.

With regard to the distinction between officers and soldiers, it is sufficient that the uniform experience of every nation of the world, combined with our own, proves the utility and propriety of the discrimination. Rewards, in proportion to the aid the public draws from them, are unquestionably due to all its servants. In some lines, the soldiers have, perhaps, generally, had an ample compensation for their sefvices, by the large bounties which have been paid them, as their officers will receive in the proposed commutation, in others, if, besides the donation of land, the payment of arreages of clothing

and wages (in which articles all the component parts
of the army must be put upon the same footing), we
take into the estimate the bounties many of the
soldiers have received, and the gratuity of one year's
full pay, which is promised to all, possibly their
situation (every circumstance being duly considered)
will not be deemed less eligible than that of the
officers.   Should a farther reward, however, be
judged equitable, I will venture to assert, no man
will enjoy greater satisfaction than myself in an
exemption from taxes for a limited time (which has
been petitioned for in some instances), or any other
adequate immunity or compensation granted to the
brave defenders of their country's cause. But neither
the adoption or rejection of this proposition will, in
any manner, affect, much less militate against the
act of Congress, by which they have offered five
years' full pay, in lieu of the half pay for life, which
had been before promised to the officers of the
army.

Before I conclude the subject on public justice, I
cannot omit to mention the obligations this country
is under to that meritorious class of veterans, the
non-commissioned officers and privates, who have
been discharged for inability, in consequence of the
resolution of Congress, of the 23d of April, 1782, on
an annual pension for life. Their peculiar sufferings, their singular merits and claims to that provision, need only to be known, to interest the feelings
of humanity in their behalf. Nothing but a punc-
tual payment of their annual allowance can rescue
them from the most complicated misery; and nothing

could be a more melancholy and distressing sight than to behold those who have shed their blood, or lost their limbs in the service of their country, without a shelter, without a friend, and without the means of obtaining any of the comforts or necessaries of life, compelled to beg their bread daily from door to door. Suffer me to recommend those of this description, belonging to your state, to the warmest patronage of your excellency and your legislature.

It is necessary to say but a few words on the third topic which was proposed, and which regards particularly the defence of the republic—as there can be little doubt but Congress will recommend a proper peace establishment for the United States, in which a due attention will be paid to the importance of placing the militia of the union upon a regular and respectable footing. If this should be the case, I should beg leave to urge the great advantage of it in the strongest terms.

The militia of this country must be considered as the palladium of our security, and the first effectual resort in case of hostility. It is essential, therefore, that the same system should pervade the whole ; that the formation and discipline of the militia of the continent should be absolutely uniform ; and that the same species of arms, accoutrement, and military apparatus, should be introduced in every part of the United States. No one, who has not learned it from experience, can conceive the difficulty, expense, and confusion, which result from a contrary system, or the vague arrangements which have hitherto prevailed.

If, in treating of political points, a greater latitude than usual has been taken in the course of the address, the importance of the crisis, and the magnitude of the objects in discussion, must be my apology. It is, however, neither my wish nor expectation, that the preceding observations should claim any regard, except so far as they shall appear to be dictated by a good intention, consonant to the immutable rules of justice ; calculated to produce a liberal system of policy, and founded on whatever experience may have been acquired by a long and close attention to public business. Here I might speak with more confidence from my actual observations; and, if it would not swell this letter (already too prolix) beyond the bounds I had prescribed myself, I could demonstrate to every mind open to conviction, that, in less time, and with much less expense than has been incurred, the war might have been brought to the same happy conclusion, if the resources of the continent could have been properly called forth ; that the distresses and disappointments which have very often occurred, have, in too many instances, resulted more from a want of energy in the continental government than a deficiency of means in the particular states ; that the inefficacy of the measures, arising from the want of an adequate authority in the supreme power, from partial compliance with the requisitions of Congress, in some of the states, and from a failure of punctuality in others, while they tended to damp the zeal of those who were more willing to exert themselves, served also to accumulate the expenses of the war, and to frustrate the best concerted plans; and that the discouragement occasioned by the complicated difficulties and embarrassments, in which our affairs were by this means involved, would have long ago produced the dissolution of any army, less patient, less virtuous and less persevering, than that which I have had the honor to command. But, while I mention those things which are notorious facts, as the defects of our federal constitution, particularly in the prosecution of a war, I beg it may be understood, that, as I have ever taken a pleasure in gratefully acknowledging the assistance and support I have derived from every class of citizens, so I shall always be happy to do justice to the unparalleled exertions of the individual states on many interesting occasions.

I have thus freely disclosed what I wished to make known before I surrendered up my public trust to those who committed it to me. The task is now accomplished; I now bid adieu to your excellency, as the chief magistrate of your state; at the same time I bid a last farewell to the cares of office, and all the employments of public life.

It remains, then, to be my final and only request, that your excellency will communicate these sentiments to your Legislature at their next meeting, and that they may be considered as the legacy of one who has ardently wished, on all occasions, to be useful to his country, and who, even in the shade of retirement, will not fail to implore the Divine benediction upon it.

I now make it my earnest prayer, that God would

have you, and the state over which you preside, in
his holy protection; that he would incline the
hearts of the citizens to cultivate a spirit of subordi-
nation and obedience to government; to entertain a
brotherly affection and love for one another; for
their fellow-citizens of the United States at large;
and particularly for their brethren who have served
in the field; and, finally, that he would most gra-
ciously be pleased to dispose us all to do justice, to
love mercy, and to demean ourselves with that
charity, humility, and pacific temper of the mind,
which were the characteristics of the Divine Author
of our blessed religion, without an humble imitation
of whose example, in these things, we can never
hope to be a happy nation.

I have the honor to be, with much esteem and respect, sir, your excellency's most obedient and most
humble servant.

GEORGE WASHINGTON.

FAREWELL TO THE ARMY.

Princeton, November 2, 1783.

THE United States in Congress assembled, after
giving the most honorable testimony to the merits of
the federal armies, and presenting them with the
thanks of their country for their long, eminent, and
faithful services, having thought proper, by their
proclamation bearing date the 18th day of October
last, to discharge such part of the troops as were
engaged for the war, and to permit the officers on

furloughs to retire from service, from and after to-morrow; which proclamation having been communicated in the public papers for the information and government of all concerned, it only remains for the Commander-in chief to address himself once more, and that for the last time, to the armies of the United States (however widely dispersed the individuals who composed them may be), and to bid them an affectionate, a long farewell.

But before the Commander-in-chief takes his final leave of those he holds most dear, he wishes to indulge himself a few moments in calling to mind a slight review of the past. He will then take the liberty of exploring with his military friends their future prospects, of advising the general line of conduct, which, in his opinion, ought to be pursued; and he will conclude the address by expressing the obligations he feels himself under for the spirited and able assistance he has experienced from them, in the performance of an arduous office.

A contemplation of the complete attainment (at a period earlier than could have been expected) of the object, for which we contended against so formidable a power, cannot but inspire us with astonishment and gratitude. The disadvantageous circumstances on our part, under which the war was undertaken, can never be forgotten. The singular interpositions of Providence in our feeble condition were such, as could scarcely escape the attention of the most unobserving; while the unparalleled perseverance of the armies of the United States, through almost every possible suffering and discouragement for the space of eight long years, was little short of a standing miracle. .

It is not the meaning nor within the compass of this address, to detail the hardships peculiarly incident to our service, or to describe the distresses which in several instances have resulted from the extremes of hunger and nakedness, combined with the rigors of an inclement season; nor is it necessary to dwell on the dark side of our past affairs. Every American officer and soldier must now console himself for any unpleasant circumstances which may have occurred, by a recollection of the uncommon scenes of which he has been called to act no inglorious part, and the astonishing events of which he has been a witness; events which have seldom, if ever before, taken place on the stage of human action nor can they probably ever happen again. For who has before seen a disciplined army formed at once from such raw materials? Who, that was not a witness, could imagine, that the most violent local prejudices would cease so soon; and that men, who came from the different parts of the continent, strongly disposed by the habits of education to despise and quarrel with each other, would instantly become but one patriotic band of brothers? Or who, that was not on the spot, can trace the steps by which such a wonderful revolution has been effected, and such a glorious period put to all our warlike toils?

It is universally acknowledged that the enlarged prospects of happiness, opened by the confirmation of our independence and sovereignty, almost exceed the power of description. And shall not the brave men, who have contributed so essentially to these inestimable acquisitions, retiring victorious from the field of war to the field of agriculture, participate in all the blessings which have been obtained? In such a republic, who will exclude them from the rights of citizens, and the fruits of their labor? In such a country, so happily circumstanced, the pursuits of commerce and the cultivation of the soil will unfold to industry the certain road to competence. To those hardy soldiers, who are actuated by the spirit of adventure, the fisheries will afford ample and profitable employment; and the extensive and fertile regions of the West will yield a most happy asylum to those who, fond of domestic enjoyment, are seeking for personal independence. Nor is it possible to conceive that any one of the United States will prefer a national bankruptcy, and a dissolution of the Union, to a compliance with the requisitions of Congress, and the payment of its just debts; so that the officers and soldiers may expect considerable assistance, in recommencing their civil occupations, from the sums due to them from the public, which must and will most inevitably be paid.

In order to effect this desirable purpose, and to remove the prejudices which may have taken possession of the minds of any of the good people of the states, it is earnestly recommended to all the troops that, with strong attachments to the Union, they should carry with them into civil society the most conciliating dispositions, and that they should prove themselves not less virtuous and useful as citizens

than they have been persevering and victorious as
soldiers. What though there should be some envious
individuals, who are unwilling to pay the debt the
public has contracted, or to yield the tribute due to
merit; yet let such unworthy treatment produce no
invectives, nor any instance of intemperate conduct.
Let it be remembered that the unbiased voice of the
free citizens of the United States has promised the
just reward and given the merited applause. Let it
be known and remembered that the reputation of the
federal armies is established beyond the reach of
malevolence; and let a consciousness of their
achievements and fame still incite the men who
composed them to honorable actions; under the per-
suasion that the private virtues of economy, prudence and industry will not be less amiable in civil
life than the more splendid qualities of valor, perseverance and enterprise were in the field. Every one
may rest assured that much, very much of the future
happiness of the officers and men will depend upon
the wise and manly conduct which shall be adopted
by them when they are mingled with the great body
of the community. And although the General has
so frequently given it as his opinion in the most
public and explicit manner that, unless the principles of the Federal Government were properly supported, and the powers of the Union increased, the
honor, dignity and justice of the nation would be
lost forever; yet he cannot help repeating on this
occasion so interesting a sentiment, and leaving it as
his last injunction to every officer and every soldier,
who may view the subject in the same serious point

of light, to add his best endeavors to those of his worthy fellow-citizens toward effecting these great and valuable purposes, on which our very existence as a nation so materially depends.

The Commander-in-chief conceives little is now wanting to enable the soldiers to change the military character into that of the citizen, but that steady and decent tenor of behavior which has generally distinguished, not only the army under his immediate command, but the different detachments and separate armies through the course of the war. From their good sense and prudence he anticipates the happiest consequences, and while he congratulates them on the glorious occasion which renders their services in the field no longer necessary, he wishes to express the strong obligations he feels himself under for the assistance he has received from every class and in every instance. He presents his thanks in the most serious and affectionate manner to the general officers, as well for their counsel on many interesting occasions, as for their ardor in promoting the success of the plans he had adopted; to the commandants of regiments and corps, and to the other officers, for their great zeal and attention in carrying his orders promptly into execution; to the staff, for their alacrity and exactness in performing the duties of their several departments; and to the non-commissioned officers and private soldiers, for their extraordinary patience and suffering, as well as their invincible fortitude in action. To the various branches of the army the General takes this last and solemn opportunity of professing his inviolable attachment and friendship. He wishes more than bare professions were in his power; that he were really able to be useful to them all in future life. He flatters himself, however, they will do him the justice to believe, that whatever could with propriety be attempted by him has been done.

And being now to conclude these his last public orders, to take his ultimate leave in a short time of the military character, and to bid a final adieu to the armies he has so long had the honor to command, he can only again offer in their behalf his recommendations to their grateful country, and his prayers to the God of armies. May ample justice be done them here, and may the choicest of Heaven's favors, both here and hereafter, attend those who, under the Divine auspices, have secured innumerable blessings for others. With these wishes and his benediction, the Commander-in-chief is about to retire from service. The curtain of separation will soon be drawn, and the military scene to him will be closed forever.

RESIGNATION OF COMMISSION.

New York, December 23, 1783.

Mr. President: The great events on which my resignation depended having at length taken place, I have now the honor of offering my sincere congratulations to Congress, and of presenting myself before them to surrender into their hands the trust committed to me, and to claim the indulgence of retiring from the service of my country.

Happy in the confirmation of our independence and sovereignty, and pleased with the opportunity afforded the United States of becoming a respectable nation, I resign, with satisfaction, the appointment I accepted with diffidence; a diffidence in my abilities to accomplish so arduous a task, which, however, was superseded by a confidence in the rectitude of our cause, the support of the Supreme Power of the Union, and the patronage of Heaven.

The successful termination of the war has verified the most sanguine expectations; and my gratitude for the interposition of Providence, and the assistance I have received from my countrymen, increases with every review of the momentous contest.

While I repeat my obligations to the army in general, I should do injustice to my own feelings not to acknowledge, in this place, the peculiar services and distinguished merits of the persons who have been attached to my person during the war. It was impossible the choice of confidential officers to compose my family could have been more fortunate. Permit me, sir, to recommend in particular those who have continued in the service to the present moment as worthy of the favorable notice and patronage of Congress.

I consider it as an indispensable duty to close this last solemn act of my official life, by commending the interests of our dearest country to the protection of Almighty God, and those who have the superintendence of them to his holy keeping.

Having now finished the work assigned me, I retire from the great theater of action; and, bidding an affectionate farewell to this august body under whose orders I have long acted, I here offer my commission, and take my leave of all the employments of public life.

INAUGURAL ADDRESS.

New York, April 30, 1789.

FELLOW CITIZENS OF THE SENATE AND OF THE HOUSE OF REPRESENTATIVES—Among the vicissitudes incident to life, no event could have filled me with greater anxieties than that, of which the notification was transmitted by your order, and received on the fourth day of the present month. On the one hand, I was summoned by my country, whose voice I can never hear but with veneration and love, from a retreat which I had chosen with the fondest predilection, and, in my flattering hopes, with an immutable decision as the asylum of my declining years; a retreat which was rendered every day more necessary as well as more dear to me, by the addition of habit to inclination, and of frequent interruptions in my health to the gradual waste committed on it by time, on the other hand, the magnitude and difficulty of the trust to which the voice of my country called me, being sufficient to awaken, in the wisest and most experienced of her citizens, a distrustful scrutiny into his qualifications, could not but overwhelm with despondence one who, inheriting inferior endowments from nature, and unpractised in the duties of civil administration, ought to be peculiarly consci-

ous of his own deficiencies. In this conflict of emo-
tions, all I dare aver is, that it has been my faithful
study to collect my duty from a just appreciation of
every circumstance by which it might be affected.
All I dare hope is, that if, in executing this task, I
have been too much swayed by a grateful remem-
brance of former instances, or by an affectionate sensibility to this transcendent proof of the confidence
of my fellow-citizens, and have thence too little con-
sulted my incapacity as well as disinclination for the
weighty and untried cares before me, my error will
be palliated by the motives which misled me, and its
consequences be judged by my country, with some
share of the partiality in which they originated.

Such being the impressions under which I have,
in obedience to the public summons, repaired to the
present station, it would be peculiarly improper to
omit, in this first official act, my fervent supplica-
tions to that Almighty Being, who rules over the
universe, who presides in the councils of nations,
and whose providential aids can supply every human
defect, that His benediction may consecrate to the
liberties and happiness of the people of the United
States, a government instituted by themselves for
these essential purposes, and may enable every instrument employed in its administration, to execute,
with success, the functions allotted to his charge.
In tendering this homage to the Great Author of
every public and private good, I assure myself that
it expresses your sentiments not less than my own;
nor those of my fellow-citizens at large less than
either. No people can be bound to acknowledge and

adore the invisible hand which conducts the affairs of men, more than the people of the United States. Every step by which they have advanced to the character of an independent nation, seems to have been distinguished by some token of providential agency. And, in the important revolution just accomplished, in the system of their united government, the tranquil deliberations and voluntary consent of so many distinct communities, from which the event has resulted, cannot be compared with the means by which most governments have been established, without some return of pious gratitude, along with an humble anticipation of the future blessings, which the past seems to presage. These reflections, arising out of the present crisis, have forced themselves too strongly on my mind to be suppressed. You will join with me, I trust, in thinking that there are none under the influence of which the proceedings of a new and free government can more auspiciously commence.

By the article establishing the executive department, it is made the duty of the president "to recommend to your consideration such measures as he shall judge necessary and expedient." The circumstances under which I now meet you will acquit me from entering into that subject farther than to refer you to the great constitutional charter under which we are assembled; and which, in defining your powers, designates the objects to which your attention is to be given. It will be more consistent with those circumstances, and far more congenial with the feelings which actuate me, to substitute, in place of a recommendation of particular measures, the tribute that is due to the talents, the rectitude, and the patriotism which adorn the characters selected to devise and adopt them. In these honorable qualifications, I behold the surest pledges, that as, on one side, no local prejudices or attachments, no separate views nor party animosities will misdirect the comprehensive and equal eye which ought to watch over this great assemblage of communities and interests—so, on another, that the foundations of our national policy will be laid in the pure and immutable principles of private morality; and the pre-eminence of a free government be exemplified by all the attributes which can win the affections of its citizens, and command the respect of the world.

I dwell on this prospect with every satisfaction which an ardent love for my country can inspire; since there is no truth more thoroughly established than that there exists, in the economy and course of nature, an indissoluble union between virtue and happiness—between duty and advantage—between the genuine maxims of an honest and magnanimous policy and the solid rewards of public prosperity and felicity—since we ought to be no less persuaded that the propitious smiles of Heaven can never be expected on a nation that disregards the eternal rules of order and right which Heaven itself has ordained —and since the preservation of the sacred life of liberty, and the destiny of the republican model of government, are justly considered as deeply, perhaps, as finally staked, on the experiment entrusted to the hands of the American people.

Besides the ordinary objects submitted to your care, it will remain with your judgment to decide how far an exercise of the occasional power delegated by the fifth article of the constitution is rendered expedient, at the present juncture, by the nature of objections which have been urged against the system or by the degree of inquietude which has given birth to them. Instead of undertaking particular recommendations on this subject, in which I could be guided by no lights derived from official opportunities, I shall again give way to my entire confidence in your discernment and pursuit of the public good. For, I assure myself, that, whilst you carefully avoid every alteration which might endanger the benefits of an united and effective government, or which ought to await the future lessons of experience, a reverence for the characteristic rights of freemen, and a regard for the public harmony, will sufficiently influence your deliberations on the question, how far the former can be more impregnably fortified, or the latter be safely and more advantageously promoted.

To the preceding observations I have one to add, which will be most properly addressed to the House of Representatives. It concerns myself, and will therefore be as brief as possible.

When I was first honored with a call into the service of my country, then on the eve of an arduous struggle for its liberties, the light in which I contemplated my duty, required that I should renounce every pecuniary compensation. From this resolution I have in no instance departed. And being still under the impression which produced it, I must decline, as inapplicable to myself, any share in the personal emoluments, which may be indispensably included in a permanent provision for the executive department: and must accordingly pray that the pecuniary estimates for the station in which I am placed, may, during my continuation in it, be limited to such actual expenditures as the public good may be thought to require.

Having thus imparted to you my sentiments, as they have been awakened by the occasion which brings us together, I shall take my present leave, but not without resorting once more to the benign Parent of the human race, in humble supplication, that, since he has been pleased to favor the American people with opportunities for deliberating in perfect tranquillity, and dispositions for deciding with unparalleled unanimity, on a form of government for the security of their union, and the advancement of their happiness, so his divine blessing may be equally conspicuous in the enlarged views, the temperate consultations, and the wise measures on which the success of this government must depend.

FAREWELL ADDRESS.

United States, September 17, 1796.

FRIENDS AND FELLOW CITIZENS—The period for a new election of a citizen, to administer the executive government of the United States, being not far distant, and the time actually arrived, when your thoughts must be employed in designating the person who is to be clothed with that important trust, it appears to me proper, especially as it may conduct to a more distinct expression of the public voice, that I should now apprise you of the resolution I have formed, to decline being considered among the number of those out of whom a choice is to be made.

I beg you, at the same time, to do me the justice to be assured, that this resolution has not been taken without a strict regard to all the considerations appertaining to the relation which binds a dutiful citizen to his country; and that, in withdrawing the tender of service, which silence in my situation might imply, I am influenced by no diminution of zeal for your future interest; no deficiency of grateful respect for your past kindness; but am supported by a full conviction that the step is compatible with both.

The acceptance of, and continuance hitherto in, the office to which your suffrages have twice called me, have been a uniform sacrifice of inclination to the opinion of duty, and to a deference for what appeared to be your desire. I constantly hoped, that it would have been much earlier in my power, consistently with motives, which I was not at liberty to disregard, to return to that retirement from which I had been reluctantly drawn. The strength of my inclination to do this, previous to the last election, had even led to the preparation of an address to declare it to you; but mature reflection on the then perplexed and critical posture of our affairs with foreign nations, and the unanimous advice of persons entitled to my confidence, impelled me to abandon the idea.

I rejoice that the state of your concerns, external

as well as internal, no longer renders the pursuit of inclination incompatible with the sentiment of duty or propriety; and am persuaded whatever partiality may be retained for my services, that, in the present circumstances of our country, you will not disapprove my determination to retire.

The impressions with which I first undertook the arduous trust were explained on the proper occasion. In the discharge of this trust I will only say that I have with good intentions contributed toward the organization and administration of the government the best exertions of which a very fallible judgment was capable. Not unconscious in the outset of the inferiority of my qualifications, experience in my own eyes, perhaps still more in the eyes of others, has strengthened the motives to diffidence of myself; and every day the increasing weight of years admonishes me more and more that the shade of retirement is as necessary to me as it will be welcome. Satisfied that if any circumstances have given peculiar value to my services, they were temporary, I have the consolation to believe that, while choice and prudence invite me to quit the political scene, patriotism does not forbid it.

In looking forward to the moment which is intended to terminate the career of my public life, my feelings do not permit me to suspend the deep acknowledgment of that debt of gratitude which I owe to my beloved country for the many honors it has conferred upon me; still more for the steadfast confidence with which it has supported me; and for the opportunities I have thence enjoyed of manifesting my inviolable attachment by services faithful and persevering, though in usefulness unequal to my zeal. If benefits have resulted to our country from these services, let it always be remembered to your praise, and as an instructive example in our annals, that under circumstances in which the passions, agitated in every direction, were liable to mislead, amidst appearances sometimes dubious, vicissitudes of fortune often discouraging, in situations in which not unfrequently want of success has countenanced the spirit of criticism, the constancy of your support was the essential prop of the efforts, and a guarantee of the plans by which they were effected. Profoundly penetrated with this idea, I shall carry it with me to my grave, as a strong incitement to unceasing vows that Heaven may continue to you the choicest tokens of its beneficence; that your union and brotherly affection may be perpetual; that the free constitution, which is the work of your hands, may be sacredly maintained; that its administration in every department may be stamped with wisdom and virtue; that, in fine, the happiness of the people of these states, under the auspices of liberty, may be made complete, by so careful a preservation and so prudent a use of this blessing, as will acquire to them the glory of recommending it to the applause, the affection and adoption of every nation, which is yet a stranger to it.

Here, perhaps, I ought to stop. But a solicitude for your welfare, which cannot end but with my life, and the apprehension of danger, natural to that solicitude, urge me, on an occasion like the present, to offer to your solemn contemplation, and to recommend to your frequent review, some sentiments, which are the result of much reflection, of no inconsiderable observation, and which appear to me all-important to the permanency of your felicity as a people. These will be offered to you with the more freedom, as you can only see in them the disinterested warnings of a parting friend, who can possibly have no personal motive to bias his counsel. Nor can I forget, as an encouragement to it, your indulgent reception of my sentiments on a former and not dissimilar occasion.

Interwoven as is the love of liberty with every ligament of your hearts, no recommendation of mine is necessary to fortify or confirm the attachment.

The unity of government, which constitutes you one people, is also now dear to you. It is justly so; for it is a main pillar in the edifice of your real independence, the support of your tranquility at home, your peace abroad; of your safety; of your prosperity; of that very liberty, which you so highly prize. But as it is easy to foresee, that from different causes and from different quarters much pains will be taken, many artifices employed, to weaken in your minds the conviction of this truth; as this is the point in your political fortress against which the batteries of internal and external enemies will be most constantly and actively (though often covertly and insidiously) directed, it is of infinite moment that you should properly estimate the immense value of your national union to your collective and individual happiness;

that you should cherish a cordial, habitual, and immovable attachment to it; accustoming yourselves to think and speak of it as of the palladium of your political safety and prosperity; watching for its preservation with jealous anxiety; discountenancing whatever may suggest even a suspicion that it can in any event be abandoned; and indignantly frowning upon the first dawning of every attempt to alienate any portion of our country from the rest, or to enfeeble the sacred ties which now link together the various parts.

For this you have every inducement of sympathy and interest. Citizens, by birth or choice, of a common country, that country has a right to concentrate your affections. The name of America, which belongs to you, in your national capacity, must always exalt the just pride of patriotism, more than any appellation derived from local discriminations. With slight shades of difference, you have the same religion, manners, habits and political principles. You have in a common cause fought and triumphed together; the independence and liberty you possess are the work of joint counsels and joint efforts, of common dangers, sufferings and successes.

But these considerations, however powerfully they address themselves to your sensibility, are greatly outweighed by those which apply more immediately to your interest. Here every portion of our country finds the most commanding motives for carefully guarding and preserving the union of the whole.

The North, in an unrestrained intercourse with the South, protected by the equal laws of a common government, finds in the productions of the latter, great additional resources of maritime and commercial enterprise and precious materials of manufacing industry. The South, in the same intercourse, benefiting by the agency of the North, see its agriculture grow and its commerce expand. Turning partly into its own channels the seamen of the North, it finds its particular navigation invigorated; and, while it contributes in different ways to nourish and increase the general mass of the national navigation, it looks forward to the protection of a maritime strength, to which itself is unequally adapted. The East, in a like intercourse with the West, already finds, and in the progressive improvement of interior communications by land and water will more and more find, a valuable vent for the commodities which it brings from abroad, or manufactures at home. The West derives from the East supplies requisite to its growth and comfort, and what is perhaps of still greater consequence, it must of necessity owe the secure enjoyment of indispensable outlets for its own productions to the weight, influence and the future maritime strength of the Atlantic side of the Union, directed by an indissoluble community of interest as one nation. Any other tenure by which the West can hold this essential advantage, whether derived from its own separate strength, or from an apostate and unnatural connection with any foreign power, must be intrinsically precarious.

While, then, in every part of our country thus feels an immediate and particular interest in union, all the parts combined cannot fail to find in the united mass of means and efforts greater strength, greater resource, proportionably greater security from external danger, a less frequent interruption of their peace by foreign nations, and, what is of inestimable value, they must derive from union an exemption from those broils and wars between themselves, which so frequently afflict neighboring countries not tied together by the same governments, which their own rivalships alone would be sufficient to produce, but which opposite foreign alliances, attachments and intrigues would stimulate and embitter. Hence, likewise, they will avoid the necessity of those overgrown military establishments, which, under any form of government, are inauspicious to liberty, and which are to be regarded as particularly hostile to republican liberty. In this sense it is, that your union ought to be considered as a main prop of your liberty, and that the love of the one ought to endear to you the preservation of the other.

These considerations speak a persuasive language to every reflecting and virtuous mind, and exhibit the continuance of the Union as a primary object of patriotic desire. Is there a doubt whether a common government can embrace so large a sphere ? Let experience solve it. To listen to mere speculation in such a case were criminal. We are authorized to hope, that a proper organization of the whole, with the auxiliary agency of governments for the respective subdivisions, will afford a happy issue to the experiment. It is well worth a fair and full experiment. With such powerful and obvious motives to union, affecting all parts of our country, while experience shall not have demonstrated its impractica、 bility, there will always be reason to distrust the patriotism of those, who in any quarter may endea- vor to weaken its bands.

In contemplating the causes which may disturb our Union, it occurs as a matter of serious concern, that any ground should have been furnished for characterizing parties by geographical discriminations Northern and Southern, Atlantic and Western; whence designing men may endeavor to excite a be- lief that there is a real difference of local interests and views. One of the expedients of party to ac- quire influence, within particular districts, is to mis- represent the opinions and aims of other districts. You cannot shield yourselves too much against the jealousies and heart-burnings, which spring from these misrepresentations; they tend to render alien to each other those who ought to be bound together by fraternal affection. The inhabitants of our west- ern country have lately had a useful lesson on this head; they have seen, in the negotiation by the Ex- ecutive, and in the unanimous ratification by the Senate, of the treaty with Spain, and in the univer- sal satisfaction at that event, throughout the United States, a decisive proof how unfounded were the suspicions propagated among them of a policy in the General Government and in the Atlantic States un- friendly to their interests in regard to the Mississippi; they have been witnesses to the formation of two treaties, that with Great Britain and that with Spain, which secure to them every thing they could desire, in respect to our foreign relations, towards confirming their prosperity. Will it not be their wisdom to rely for the preservation of these advantages on the Union by which they were procured? Will they not henceforth be deaf to those advisers, if such there are, who would sever them from their brethren and connect them with aliens?

To the efficacy and permanency of your Union, a Government for the whole is indispensable. No alliances, however strict, between the parts can be an adequate substitute; they must inevitably experience the infractions and interruptions, which all alliances in all times have experienced. Sensible of this momentous truth, you have improved upon your first essay, by the adoption of a Constitution of Government better calculated than your former for an intimate Union, and for the efficacious management of your common concerns. This Government, the offspring of our own choice, uninfluenced and unawed, adopted upon full investigation and mature deliberation, completely free in its principles, in the distribution of its powers, uniting security with energy, and containing within itself a provision for its own amendment, has a just claim to your confidence and your support. Respect for its authority, compliance with its laws, acquiescence in its measures, are duties enjoined by the fundamental maxims of true Liberty. The basis of our political systems is the right of the people to make and to alter their constitutions of government. But the constitution which at any time exists, till changed by an explicit and authentic act of the whole people, is sacredly obligatory upon all. The very idea of the power and the right of the people to establish Government presupposes the duty of every individual to obey the established Government.

All obstructions to the execution of the laws, all combinations and associations, under whatever plausible character, with the real design to direct, control, counteract, or awe the regular deliberation and action of the constituted authorities, are destructive of this fundamental principle, and of fatal tendency. They serve to organize faction, to give it an artificial and extraordinary force; to put, in the place of the delegated will of the nation, the will of a party, often a small but artful and enterprising minority of the community; and, according to the alternate triumphs of different parties, to make the public administration the mirror of the ill-concerted and incongruous projects of faction, rather than the organ of consisted and wholesome plans digested by common counsels, and modified by mutual interests.

However combinations or associations of the above description may now and then answer popular ends, they are likely in the course of time and things, to become potent engines, by which cunning, ambitious, and unprincipled men will be enabled to subvert the power of the people, and to usurp for themselves the reins of government; destroying afterwards the very engines which have lifted them to unjust dominion.

Towards the preservation of your government, and the permanency of your present happy state, it is requisite, not only that you steadily discountenance irregular oppositions to its acknowledged au-

thority, but also that you resist with care the spirit
of innovation upon its principles, however specious
the pretexts. One method of assault may be to
effect, in the forms of the constitution, alterations,
which will impair the energy of the system, and
thus to undermine what cannot be directly over-
thrown. In all the changes to which you may be
invited, remember that time and habit are at least
as necessary to fix the true character of governments,
as of other human institutions; that experience is
the surest standard by which to test the real tendency of the existing constitution of a country; that
facility in changes, upon the credit of mere hypothesis and opinion, exposes to perpetual change, from
the endless variety of hypothesis and opinion; and
remember, especially, that, for the efficient management of your common interests, in a country so extensive as ours, a government of as much vigor as is
consistent with the perfect security of liberty is indispensable. Liberty itself will find in such a government, with powers properly distributed and ad-
justed, its surest guardian. It is, indeed, little else
than a name, where the government is too feeble to
withstand the enterprises of faction, to confine each
member of the society within the limits prescribed
by the laws, and to maintain all in the secure and
tranquil enjoyment of the rights of person and property.

I have already intimated to you the danger of parties in the state, with particular reference to the
founding of them on geographical discrimination.
Let me now take a more comprehensive view, and

warn you in the most solemn manner against the baneful effects of the spirit of party, generally.

This spirit, unfortunately, is inseparable from our nature, having its root in the strongest passions of the human mind. It exists under different shapes in all governments, more or less stifled, controlled, or repressed; but, in those of the popular form it is seen in its greatest rankness, and is truly their worst enemy.

The alternate domination of one faction over another, sharpened by the spirit of revenge, natural to party dissension, which in different ages and countries has perpetrated the most horrid enormities, is itself a frightful despotism. But this *leads* at length to a more formal and permanent despotism. The disorders and miseries, which result, gradually incline the minds of men to seek security and repose in the absolute power of an individual; and sooner or later the chief of some prevailing faction, more able or more fortunate than his competitors, turns this disposition to the purposes of his own elevation, on the ruins of public liberty.

Without looking forward to an extremity of this kind (which nevertheless ought not to be entirely out of sight), the common and continual mischiefs of the spirit of party are sufficient to make it the interest and duty of a wise people to discourage and restrain it.

It serves always to distract the public councils, and enfeeble the public administration. It agitates the community with ill-founded jealousies and false alarms; kindles the animosity of one part against another, foments occasionally riot and insurrection. It opens the doors to foreign influence and corruption, which find a facilitated access to the government itself through the channels of party passions. Thus the policy and the will of one country are subjected to the policy and will of another.

There is an opinion, that parties in free countries are useful checks upon the administration of the government, and serve to keep alive the spirit of liberty. This within certain limits is probably true, and in governments of a monarchical cast, patriotism may look with indulgence, if not with favor, upon the spirit of party. But in those of the popular character, in governments purely elective, it is a spirit not to be encouraged. From their natural tendency, it is certain there will always be enough of that spirit far every salutary purpose. And, there being constant danger of excess, the effort ought to be, by force of public opinion to mitigate and assuage it. A fire not to be quenched, it demands a uniform vigilance to prevent its bursting into a flame, lest, instead of warming, it should consume.

It is important, likewise, that the habits of thinking in a free country should inspire caution, in those intrusted with its administration, to confine themselves within their respective constitutional spheres, avoiding in the exercise of the powers of one department to encroach upon another. The spirit of encroachment tends to consolidate the powers of all the departments in one, and thus to create, whatever the form of government, a real despotism. A just estimate of that love of power, and proneness to abuse it, which predominates in the human heart, is sufficient to satisfy us of the truth of this position. The necessity of reciprocal checks in the exercise of political power, by dividing and distributing it into different depositories, and constituting each the guardian of the public weal against invasions by the others, has been evinced by experiments ancient and modern; some of them in our country and under our own eyes. To preserve them must be as necessary as to institute them. If, in the opinion of the people, the distribution or modification of the constitutional powers be in any particular wrong, let it be corrected by an amendment in the way which the constitution designates. But let there be no change by usurpation; for, though this, in one instance, may be the instrument of good, it is the customary weapon by which free governments are destroyed. The precedent must always greatly overbalance in permanent evil any partial or transient benefit, which the use can at any time yield.

Of all the dispositions and habits, which lead to political prosperity, religion and morality are indispensable supports. In vain would that man claim the tribute of patriotism, who should labor to subvert these great pillars of human happiness, these firmest props of the duties of men and citizens. The mere politician equally with the pious man, ought to respect and to cherish them. A volume could not trace all their connexions with private and public felicity. Let it simply be asked, Where is the security for property, for reputation, for life, if the sense of religious obligation desert the oaths, which are the instruments of investigation in courts of justice? And let us with caution indulge the supposition, that morality can be maintained without religion. Whatever may be conceded to the influence of refined education on minds of peculiar structure, reason and experience both forbid us to expect, that national morality can prevail in exclusion of religious principle.

It is substantially true that virtue or morality is a necessary spring of popular government. The rule, indeed, extends with more or less force to every species of free government. Who, that is a sincere friend to it, can look with indifference upon attempts to shake the foundation of the fabric?

Promote, then, as an object of primary importance institutions for the general diffusion of knowledge. In proportion as the structure of a government gives force to public opinion, it is essential that public opinion should be enlightened.

As a very important source of strength and security, cherish public credit. One method of preserving it is, to use it as sparingly as possible; avoiding occasions of expense by cultivating peace, but remembering also that timely disbursements to prepare for danger frequently prevent much greater disbursements to repel it; avoiding likewise the accumulation of debt, not only by shunning occasions of expense, but by vigorous exertion in time of peace to discharge the debts, which unavoidable wars may have occasioned not ungenerously throwing upon posterity the burden which we ourselves ought to bear. The execution of these maxims belongs to your representatives, but it is necessary that public opinion should co-operate. To facilitate to them the performance of their duty it is essential that you should practically bear in mind, that towards the payment of debts there must be revenue; that to have revenue there must be taxes; that no taxes can be devised which are not more or less inconvenient and unpleasant; that the intrinsic embarrassment, inseparable from the selection of the proper objects (which is always a choice of difficulties), ought to be a decisive motive for a candid construction of the conduct of the government in making it, and for a spirit of acquiescence in the measures for obtaining revenue, which the public exigencies may at any time dictate.

Observe good faith and justice towards all nations; cultivate peace and harmony with all. Religion and morality enjoin this conduct; and can it be, that good policy does not equally enjoin it? It will be worthy of a free, enlightened, and at no distant period, a great nation, to give to mankind the magnanimous and too novel example of a people always guided by an exalted justice and benevolence. Who can doubt, that in the course of time and things, the fruits of such a plan would richly repay any temporary advantages, which might be lost by a steady adherence to it? Can it be that Providence has not connected the permanent felicity of a nation with its virtue? The experiment, at least, is recommended by every sentiment which ennobles human nature. Alas! is it rendered impossible by its vices?

In the execution of such a plan, nothing is more

essential, than that permanent, inveterate antipathies against particular nations, and passionate attachments for others, should be excluded; and that, in place of them, just and amicable feelings towards all should be cultivated. The nation, which indulges towards another an habitual hatred, or an habitual fondness, is in some degree a slave. It is a slave to its animosity or to its affection, either of which is sufficient to lead it astray from its duty and its interest. Antipathy in one nation against another disposes each more readily to offer insult and injury, to lay hold of slight causes of umbrage, and to be haughty and intractable, when accidental or trifling occasions of dispute occur. Hence, frequent collisions, obstinate, envenomed, and bloody contests. The nation, prompted by ill-will and resentment, sometimes impels to war the Government, contrary to the best calculations of policy. The Government sometimes participates in the national propensity, and adopts through passion what reason would reject; at other times, it makes the animosity of the nation subservient to projects of hostility instigated by pride, ambition, and other sinister and pernicious motives. The peace often, sometimes perhaps the liberty, of nations has been the victim.

So likewise, a passionate attachment of one nation for another produces a variety of evils. Sympathy for the favorite nation, fecilitating the illusion of an imaginary common interest in cases where no real common interest exists, and infusing into one the enmities of the other, betrays the former into a participation in the quarrels and wars of the latter, without adequate inducement or justification. It leads also to concessions to the favorite nation of privileges denied to others, which is apt doubly to injure the nation making the concessions; by unnecessarily parting with what ought to have been retained; and by exciting jealousy, ill-will, and a disposition to retaliate, in the parties from whom equal privileges are withheld. And it gives to ambitious, corrupted, or deluded citizens (who devote themselves to the favorite nation), facility to betray or sacrifice the interests of their own country, without odium, sometimes even with popularity; gilding with the appearances of a virtuous sense of obligation, a commendable deference for public opinion, or a laudable zeal for public good, the base or foolish compliances of ambition, corruption or infatuation.

As avenues to foreign influence in innumerable ways, such attachments are particularly alarming to the truly enlightened and independent patriot. How many opportunities do they afford to tamper with domestic factions, to practice the arts of seduction, to mislead public opinion, to influence or awe the public councils! Such an attachment of a small or weak, towards a great and powerful nation, dooms the former to be the satellite of the latter.

Against the insidious wiles of foreign influence (I conjure you to believe me, fellow-citizens), the jealousy of a free people ought to be constantly awake, since history and experience prove that foreign influence is one of the most baneful foes of republican goverment. But that jealously, to be useful, must be impartial; else it becomes the instrument of the very influence be avoided, instead of a defence against it.   Excessive partiality for one foreign nation, and excessive dislike of another, cause those whom they actuate to see danger only on one side, and serve to veil and even second the arts of influence on the other.   Real patriots who may resist the intrigues of the favorite, are liable to become suspected and odious; while its tools and dupes usurp the applause and confidence of the purpose, to surrender their interests.

The great rule of conduct for us, in regard to foreign nations, is, in extending our commercial relations, to have with them as little political connexion as possible.   So far as we have already formed engagements, let them be fulfilled with perfect good faith.   Here let us stop.

Europe has a set of primary interests, which to us have none, or a very remote relation.   Hence she must be engaged in frequent controversies, the causes of which are essentially foreign to our concerns. Hence, therefore, it must be unwise in us to implicate ourselves, by artificial ties, in the ordinary vicissitudes of her politics, or the ordinary combinations and collisions of her friendships or enmities.

Our detached and distant situation invites and enables us to pursue a different course.   If we remain one people, under an efficient government, the period is not far off when we may defy material injury from external annoyance; when we may take such an attitude as will cause the neutrality, we may at any time resolve upon, to be scrupulously respected; when belligerent nations, under the impossibility of

making acquisitions upon us, will not lightly hazard
the giving us provocation; when we may choose
peace or war, as our interest, guided by justice shall
counsel.

Why forego the advantages of so peculiar a situation? Why quit our own to stand upon foreign
ground. Why, by interweaving our destiny with
that of any part of Europe, entangle our peace and
prosperity in the toils of European ambition, rivalship, interest, humor or caprice?

It is our true policy to steer clear of permanent alliances with any portion of the foreign world; so
far, I mean, as we are now at liberty to do it; for let
me not be understood as capable of patronizing infidelity to existing engagements. I hold the maxim
no less applicable to public than to private affairs,
that honesty is always the best policy. I repeat it,
therefore, let those engagements be observed in their
genuine sense. But, in my opinion, it is unnecessary
and would be unwise to extend them.

Taking care always to keep ourselves, by suitable
establishments, on a respectable defensive posture,
we may safely trust to temporary alliances for extraordinary emergencies.

Harmony, liberal intercourse with all nations, are
recommended by policy, humanity, and interest.
But even our commercial policy should hold an equal
and impartial hand; neither seeking nor granting
exclusive favors or preferences; consulting the natural course of things; diffusing and diversifying by
gentle means the streams of commerce, but forcing
nothing; establishing with powers so disposed, in

order to give trade a stable course, to define the rights of our merchants, and to enable the government to support them, conventional rules of intercourse, the best that present circumstances and mutual opinion will permit, but temporary, and liable to be from time to time abandoned or varied, as experience and circumstances shall dictate; constantly keeping in view, that it is folly in one nation to look for disinterested favors from another; that it must pay with a portion of its independence for whatever it may accept under that character; that, by such acceptance, it may place itself in the condition of having given equivalents for nominal favors, and yet of being reproached with ingratitude for not giving more. There can be no greater error than to expect or calculate upon real favors from nation to nation. It is an illusion, which experience must cure, which a just pride ought to discard.

In offering to you, my countrymen, these counsels of an old and affectionate friend, I dare not hope they will make the strong and lasting impression I could wish; that they will control the usual current of the passions, or prevent our nation from running the course, which has hitherto marked the destiny of nations. But, if I may even flatter myself, that they may be productive of some partial benefit, some occasional good; that they may now and then recur to moderate the fury of party spirit, to warn against the mischiefs of foreign intrigue, to guard against the impostures of pretended patriotism; this hope will be a full recompense for the solicitude for your welfare, by which they have been dictated.

How far in the discharge of my official duties I have been guided by the principles which have been delineated, the public records and other evidences of my conduct must witness to you and to the world. To myself, the assurance of my own conscience is, that I have at least believed myself to be guded by them.

In relation to the still subsisting war in Europe, my proclamation of the 22d of April, 1793, is the index of my plan. Sanctioned by your approving voice, and by that of your Representatives in both Houses of Congress, the spirit of that measure has continually governed me, uninfluenced by any attempts to deter or divert me from it.

After deliberate examination, with the aid of the best lights I could obtain, I was well satisfied that our country, under all the circumstances of the case, had a right to take, and was bound in duty and interest to take, a neutral position. Having taken it, I determined, as far as should depend upon me, to maintain it, with moderation, perseverance and firmness.

The considerations which respect the right to hold this conduct, it is not necessary on this occasion to detail. I will only observe, that, according to my understanding of the matter, that right, so far from being denied by any of the belligerent powers, has been virtually admitted by all.

The duty of holding a neutral conduct may be inferred, without anything more, from the obligation which justice and humanity impose on every nation, in cases in which it is free to act, to maintain inviolate the relations of peace and amity towards other nations.

The inducements of interest for observing that conduct will best be referred to your own reflections and experience. With me a predominant motive has been to endeavor to gain time to our country to settle and mature its yet recent institutions, and to progress without interruption to that degree of strength and consistency, which is necessary to give it, humanly speaking, the command of its own fortunes.

Though, in reviewing the incidents of my administration, I am unconscious of intentional error, I am nevertheless too sensible of my defects not to think it probable that I may have committed many errors. Whatever they may be I fervently beseech the Almighty to avert or mitigate the evils to which they may tend. I shall also carry with me the hope that my country will never cease to view them with indulgence; and that, after forty-five years of my life dedicated to its service with an upright zeal, the faults of incompetent abilities will be consigned to oblivion, as myself must soon be to the mansions of rest.

Relying on its kindness in this as in other things, and actuated by that fervent love towards it, which is so natural to a man, who views in it the native soil of himself and his progenitors for several generations; I anticipate with pleasing expectation that retreat, in which I promise myself to realize, without alloy, the sweet enjoyment of partaking, in the midst of my fellow-citizens, the benign influence of good laws under a free government, the ever favorite object of my heart, and the happy reward, as I trust, of our mutual cares, labors, and dangers.

GEORGE WASHINGTON.

NEW PRICE LIST.

BIOGRAPHY.

Eminent Americans: Brief Biographies of States. men, Patriots, Orators, and others, Men and Women, eminent in American history. By Benson J. Lossing, LL. D., author of "The History of the United States", "Field Book of the Revolution", etc. With over 100 fine portraits. A New edition. Large 12mo., Brevier type, about 500 pages. Price in cloth 70 cts.

Surveyor Boy and President. Young People's Life of George Washington. By William M. Thayer. Elzevir edition, 466 pages, Brevier type, leaded. With illustrations. Extra cloth, 50 cts.

The Pioneer Boy. Young People's Life of Abra- ham Lincoln: or, From Pioneer Home to the White House. By William M. Thayer. With Eulogy by Hon. George Bancroft. Large 12mo., 469 pages, Small Pica type, leaded. With two steel portraits, and other fine illustrations. Extra cloth 65 cts.

From Log Cabin to the White House. Young People's Life of James A. Garfield: or From Log Cabin to the White House. By William M. Thayer. With Eulogy by Hon. James G. Blaine. Large 12mo., 483 pages, Small Pica type, leaded. With two steel portraits, and other fine illustrations. Extra cloth, 65 cts.

English Men of Letters. Vol. I. Containing Chaucer, by Prof. A. W. Ward; Burns, by Principal Shair; Spenser, by the Dean of St. Paul's; Scott, by R. H. Hutto; Milton, by Mark Pattison. 12mo., Brevier type, 756 pages. Cloth, 70 cts.; half Russia, 85 cts.

English Men of Letters. Vol. II. Containin : Johnson, by Leslie Stephen; Wordsworth, by J Myers ;Goldsmith, by William Black; Shelley, by J. A. Symonds; Pope, by Leslie Stephen; Cowper, by Goldwin Smith; Southey, b Prof. Dowden. 12mo., Brevier type, 784 pages. Cloth ,70 cts.; half Russia, 85 cts.

English Men of Letters. Vol. III. Containing: Locke, by Thomas Fowler; Hume, by Prof. Huxley; De Fo , by William Minto; Gibbon, by J. C. Morrison; Burke, by John Morley; Thackeray, by Anthony Trollope; Bunyan, by J. A Froude. 12mo., Brevier type, 842 pages. Cloth, 70 cts., half Russia, 85 cts.

Achievements of Celebrated Men. By James Parton. Containing sketches of the lives of over one hundred of the most successful men of ancient and modern times. Large octavo, 839 pages, Small Pica type Cloth, $1.40.

Plutarch's Lives of Illustrious Men. Translated by Dryden and Clough. The best American edition. Three vols. large 12mo., 1,717 pages, Long Primer type. Cloth, $1.60.

Famous Biography. Twelve Books in one vol- ume. Containing; Macaulay's Life of Frederick the Great; Carlyle's Robert Burns; Lamartine's Mary Queen of Scots; Gibbon's Mahomet; Bunsen's Luther; Michelet's Joan of Arc; Arnold's Hannibal; Liddell's Cæsar; Lamartine's Cromwell; Macaulay's William Pitt; Lamartine's Columbus; Trollope's Vittoria Colonna. 12mo., 788 pages, Brevier type. Cloth, 65c.

NEW PRICE LIST.—Continued.

Frederick the Great. By T. B. Macaulay. Elzevir edition. 134 pages, Brevier type, leaded. Cloth, 20 cts.

Life of Alexander H. Stephens. By Frank H. Norton, author of "The Life of Gen. Winfield S. Hancock." Two illustrations. Elzevir edition, 94 pages, Brevier type, leaded. Cloth, 25 cts.

Life of Peter Cooper. By C. Edwards Lester. With illustrations. Elzevir edition, 116 pages, Brevier type, leaded. Extra cloth, 25 cts.

Life and Achievements of Sam Houston, Hero and Statesman. By C. Edwards Lester, author of "Life of Peter Cooper," etc. With fine portrait. Elzevir edition, 240 pages, Brevier type, leaded. Cloth, 30 cts.

FICTION.

Charles Dickens' Complete Works. New Caxton illustrated edition, 15 vols, cloth, ink and gold designs; each volume containing over 800 pages. About 200 illustrations. Long Primer type. Price per set, $9. Separate volumes, 65 cts. each.

Thackeray's Complete Works. New Caxton Illustrated edition, 11 vols., cloth, ink and gold designs; each volume containing about 800 pages about 200 illustrations. Long Primer type. Price per set, $6.75. Separate volumes, 65 cts. each.

Scott's Waverley Novels. New Caxton Illustrated edition, uniform in size, type, and binding, with Dickens and Thackeray. 12 vols., cloth. Each volume contains about 900 pages. profusely illustrated. Long Primer type. Price per set, $7.50.

George Eliot's Complete Works. New Caxton edition, uniform in all respects with Dickens, Thackeray, and Scott. 6 vols., cloth. Each volume contains over 700 pages. Long Primer type. Price per set, $3.75.

Hawthorne's Complete Works. New Globe Edition, 5 vols., cloth, 12mo.; the whole containing over 6,000 pages, with 24 fine illustrations. Long Primer type, leaded. Price per set, $6.50.

J. Fenimore Cooper's Complete Works. Globe edition, complete in 16 vols., 12mo., cloth, the whole aggregating over 15,400 pages, with 32 original illustrations by Darley, Dielman, Fredericks, Sheppard, and Waud. Long Primer type, leaded. Price per set, $12.50.

Thomas De Quincey's Complete Works. Globe edition, complete in 6 vols., 12mo., cloth, the whole aggregating over 7,500 pages. Long Primer type, leaded. Price per set, $5.50.

Sir E. Bulwer Lytton's Complete Works. New Caxton edition, uniform in all respects with Dickens, Thackeray, Waverley, Eliot, and Irving. 13 vols, cloth, ink and gold designs. Price per set, $8.50.

Works of William Black. New Caxton Edition Uniform in all respects with Dickens, Thackeray, Waverley, Eliot and Irving. In 6 vols.; handsomely bound in cloth, with ink and gold designs. Price per set, $4.

2

Works of Washington Irving. New Caxton Edi-
tion. (Complete, omitting Life of Washington.) Uniform in
all respects with Dickens, Thackeray, Waverley, etc. 6 vols.,
cloth, each volume containing over 800 pages. Price per set, $4

The following works are uniform, 12mo.
volumes, printed in Long Primer or larger
type, unless otherwise stated.

Hyperion. By H. W. Longfellow. 274 pages.
Cloth, 35 cts.

A Princess of Thule. By Wiliam Black, 464 pages.
Cloth, 40 cts.

Hyperion and Thule, in one volume, 738 pages.
Cloth, 60 cts.; half Russia, 75 cts.

Adam Bede. By George Eliot. 484 pages. Cloth,
40 cts.

Hypatia. By Charles Kingsley. 460 pages. Cloth,
40 cts.

Adam Bede and Hypatia, in one vol., 944 pages.
Cloth, 70 cts., half Russia, 85 cts.

Ivanhoe. By Sir Walter Scott. 460 pages. Cloth,
40 cts.

Last Days of Pompeii. By Sir E. Bulwer Lyt-
ton. 393 pages. Cloth, 40 cts.

Ivanhoe and Last Days of Pompeii, in one vol.,
858 pages. Cloth, 60 cts.; half Russia, 75 cts.

The Spy. By J. Fenimore Cooper. 406 pages.
Cloth, 35 cts.

Green Mt. Boys. By Judge Thompson 370 pages.
Cloth, 35 cts.

The Spy and Green Mt. Boys, in one vol., 776
pages. Cloth, 60 cts.; half Russia, 75 cts.

The Berber. By W. S. Mayo. 300 pages. Cloth,
35 cts

Horseshoe Robinson. By J. P. Kennedy, 554
pages. Cloth, 40 cts.

The Berber and Horseshoe Robinson, in one vol.,
854 pages. Cloth, 60 cts., half Russia, 75 cts.

Jane Eyre. By Charlotte Bronte, 392 pages.
Cloth, 40 cts.

John Halifax, Gentleman. By Mrs. Mulock-
Craik. 424 pages. Cloth, 40 cts.

Jane Eyre and John Halifax, in one volume, 816
pages. Cloth, 60 cts.; half Russia, 75 cts.

Vanity Fair. By Wm. M. Thackeray. Nearly
200 illustrations 774 pages. Cloth, 70 cts. 3

David Copperfield. By Charles Dickens. 854
pages. Cloth, 60 cts.; half Russia, 75 cts.

The Moonstone. By Wilkie Collins. 445 pages.
Cloth, 35 cts.

East Lynne. By Mrs. Henry Wood. 409 pages.
Cloth, 35 cts.

The Moonstone and East Lynne, in one vol., 854
pages. Cloth, 60 cts.; half Russia, 75 cts.

Wilhelm Meister. By Goethe. Translated by John
Carlyle. 596 pages. Cloth, 45 cts.; half Russia, 60 cts.

HISTORY.

Grote's History of Greece, from the Earliest Pe-
riod to the close of the generation contemporary with Alexander the Great. By George Grote. Complete in 4 vols., large
12mo., 3,355 pages, Brevier type. Price per set cloth, $2 70.

History of England, from the Invasion of Julius
Cæsar to the Revolution of 1688. By David Hume. A new
edition, with the author's latest corrections and improve-
ments, prefixed by a short account of his life, written by
himself. With a fine steel portrait. In 6 vols., octavo, 3,472
pages, Pica type. Printed on fine heavy paper. Extra cloth,
gilt top. Price per set, $6.

A cheaper edition, on lighter but excellent paper, bound in
three volumes, half Russia, red edges, $4.50; cloth, $3.75.

Macauley's History of England. New, unabridged
edition, complete in three vols., large 12mo., 2,142 pages, Brevier type. Price per set, cloth, $1.60.

Larger History of the English People. By John
Richard Green. Elzevir edition, in 5 vols., Brevier type,
leaded, 2,426 pages. Per set, cloth, $1.75.

History of the Thirty Years' War in Germany.
By Frederick Schiller. Translated by J. A. W. Morrison. Elzevir edition, Brevier type, leaded, 518 pages. Cloth, 40 cts.

Fifteen Decisive Battles of the World, from Mara-
thon to Waterloo. By E. S. Creasy. New Elzevir edition, Brevier type, leaded, 439 pages. Cloth, 40 cts.

History of the French Revolution. By Thomas
Carlyle. Elzevir edition, Brevier type, leaded, 1,228 pages.
Two vols., cloth, per set, 80 cts.

Historical "Wonder-Book." The Histories of
Green, Schiller, Creasy, and Carlyle, as above, in one volume.
Model octavo, large Brevier type, beautifully printed and
bound. 1,005 pages. Half Russia, red edges, $1.50.

Rollins' Ancient History of the Egyptians, Cartha-
genians, Assyrians, Babylonians, Medes and Persians, Gre-
cians, and Macedonians. By Charles Rollins. 4 vols., large
12mo., Long Primer type, 3,076 pages. Cloth, $2.70.

History of the Decline and Fall of the Roman
Empire. By Edward Gibbon. Complete in two vols., large
12mo., Bourgeois type, 1,958 pages. Cloth, per set, $1.7. **4**

The Notes of Dean Milman to Gibbon's Rome, as above, large 12mo., Brevier, 972 pages. Cloth 70 cts.

Ancient Egypt under the Pharaohs. By John Kenrick, M.A. Two vols., in one large 12mo., Long Primer type, 902 pages, with illustrations. Cloth, $1.

JUVENILES.

All large 12mo. vols., unless otherwise stated.

Rasselas, by Samuel Johnson; the Vickar of Wake field, by Oliver Goldsmith; Paul and Virginia, by St. Pierre. Bound in one vol., Long Primer type, 366 pages. Cloth, 45 cts.

Gulliver's Travels, by Dean Swift, and the Ad- ventures of Baron Munchausen. Bound in one volume, Long Primer type, 460 pages. Cloth, 45 cts.

Child's History of England. By Charles Dickens. Long Primer type, 362 pages. Cloth, 45 cts.

Child's History of France. By Charlotte M. Yonge. Long Primer type, 288 pages. Cloth, 45 cts.

Child's History of Germany. By Charlotte M. Yonge. Long Primer type, 310 pages. Cloth, 45 cts.

Robinson Crusoe. Brevier type, 398 pages, with numerous illustrations. Cloth, 45 cts.

The Arabian Nights. Brevier type, 386 pages. with numerous illustrations. Cloth, 45 cts.

Bunyan's Pilgrim's Progress. Bourgeois type, leaded, 316 pages, with numerous illustrations by Barnard. Cloth, 45 cts.

Æsop's Fables, complete, with text based upon Croxall, LaFontaine, and L'Estrange, with copious additions from other modern authors, profusely illustrated by Ernest Griset. Over 300 pages. Cloth, 45 cts.

Stories and Ballads for Young Folks. By Ellen Tracy Alden. A collection of stories in Prose and stories in Ballads, with short Poems, Rhymes, and Jingles. With very beautiful illustrations by Hopkins. Fine, heavy paper, elegantly printed and richly bound in cloth, black and gold. Price, 50 cts.

Cecil's Natural History. Profusely Illustrated. Part I.—Beasts. Part II.—Birds. Part III.—Insects. In one volume. By S. H. Peabody, Regent of Illinois Industrial University. Large 12mo., Small Pica type, leaded. Bound in cloth, 85 cts.

Hans Andersen's Stories. With numerous illus- trations. Elzevir edition, Long Primer type, leaded. Eight volumes bound in four. Extra cloth, price per volume, 30 cts.; per set, $1.20.

> 1. The Story-Teller and other Tales; Fairy Tales. 320 pages.
> 2. Shoes of Fortune, and other Tales; The Christmas Greeting. 336 pages.
> 8. The Ice Maiden and Other Tales; The Picture Book without Pictures, and Other Tales. 324 pages. 5

4. The Ugly Duck and Other Tales; The Mud King's Daughter, and other Tales. 320 pages.

Greenwood Juveniles. With numerous illustrations. Elzevir edition. Small Pica type, leaded. Eight volumes. Price per volume, 35 cts.; per set, $2.50.

History of my Pets, 168 pages
Recollections of my Childhood, 192 pages.
Stories from Famous Ballads, 182 pages.
Stories and Legends of Travel and History, 288 pages.
Merrie England, 262 pages.
Bonnie Scotland, 280 pages.
Stories and Sights of France and Italy, 292 pages.
Stories of Many Lands, 216 pages.

RELIGIOUS LITERATURE.

Seekers after God. By Canon F. W. Farrar.
Large 12mo., Long Primer type, leaded, 306 pages. Cloth, 35 cts.

The Hermits. By Rev. Charles Kingsley, Author
of "Hypatia," "Westward, Ho," etc. Large 12mo., Small Pica type, leaded, 340 pages. Cloth, 35 cts.

Life and Epistles of St. Paul. By Conybeare and
Howson. Large 12mo., Bourgeois type, 764 pages. Cloth, 70 cts.

The Early Days of Christianity. By Canon F. W.
Farrar. Large 12mo.. Long Primer type, The best American edition. with the author's notes, and index, complete. Cloth, 65 cts.

The Life and Words of Christ. By Cunningham
Geikie, D.D. One volume, large 12mo., Brevier type, 838 pages. Cloth, 60 cts.

Works of Flavius Josephus, comprising the An-
tiquities of the Jews, a history of the Jewish wars, and a life of Josephus, written by himself; also dissertations concerning Jesus Christ, John the Baptist, James the Just, God's Command to Abraham, etc. Translated by Wm. Whiston, together with numerous explanatory notes, a complete index, etc. In one large octavo volume, 830 double-column pages. Cloth, $1.40.

History of the Reformation. By D'Aubigne. In
one large quarto volume, Long Primer type, 751 pages, illustrated with about 200 engravings on wood. Cloth, $1.50.

The Works of John Bunyan, containing the Pil-
grim's Progress, the Holy War, Grace Abounding, the Jerusalem Sinner Saved, the Saint's Privilege, the Water of Life, and the Barren Fig Tree. With a life of Bunyan by Rev Dr. Cheever, and an Essay by James Montgomery. Illustrated with 100 engravings on wood, and a steel portrait. Large quarto, Pica type, 840 pages. Cloth, $1.50.

Legends of the Patriarchs and Prophets. By
S. Baring-Gould. Large 12mo., 450 pages, Long Primer type. Cloth, 40 cts.

MISCELLANEOUS.

Cyclopedia of Expression. Words Classified
according to their meaning, as an aid to the expression of
thought. By P. M. & J. L. Roget. New edition, large 12mo.,
742 pages. Half Russia, 90 cts.

Critical, Historical, and Miscellaneous Essays
and Poems. By Thomas Babbington Macaulay. The most
complete edition published. Three vols., large 12mo., 2,463
pages, Long Primer type. Cloth, $2.

Choice Literature, Vol. I., 496 pages, February—
August, 1883. Cloth, 75 cts.

The Adventures of Don Quixote de la Mancha.
By Cervantes. Translated by Mottoux. 16 characteristic
illustrations by Hopkins. Large 12mo., Brevier type, 612
pages. Cloth, 60 cts.

Choice Prose. Complete in one volume, Model
octavo, 292 pages, Brevier type, containing: Complete Essays;
and Wisdom of the Ancients, etc., by Lord Bacon; The complete "Letters of Junius;" Rip Van Winkle, and other
Sketches, by Washington Irving; The Words of Washington;
Life of Frederick the Great, by T. B. Macaulay; etc. Price in
cloth, 60 cts.

Doré's Bible Gallery. Large quarto, 52 cartoons
and portrait of the artist, with descriptive text by Pollard.
Printed on heavy plate paper, and elegantly bound in cloth,
$1.75.

The Choice of Books. By Charles F. Richardson,
Prof. of English Literature in Dartmouth College. New Acme
edition, 208 pages, Small Pica type, leaded. Extra cloth, 25
cts.; gilt edges, ornamented, 35 cts.

Heroes, Hero Worship, and the Heroic in History.
By Thomas Carlyle. Large 12 mo., 184 pages, Brevier type.
Cloth, 30 cts.

The Koran of Mohammed. Translated by George
Sale. Large 12mo., 336 pages, Brevier type. Cloth, 40 cts.

American Humorists: Containing Personal
Sketches, and Choice specimens from the writings of Irving,
Holmes, Lowell, Artemus Ward, Mark Twain, and Bret Harte.
By H. R. Haweis. Cloth, 25 cts.

The Cricket on the Hearth. By Charles Dick-
ens. Illustrated by Leech. Cloth, 25 cts.

Highways of Literature. By David Pryde.
Cloth, 25 cts.

The Complete Essays of Lord Bacon, with the
Notes of Joseph Devey, M.A., a New Elzevir edition, Brevier
type, leaded, 217 pages. Cloth, 25 cts.

Sayings, Wise and Otherwise. By the author of
"Sparrowgrass Papers," with an autobiographic sketch and
an introductory note by Donald G. Mitchell (Ike Marvel).
16 mo. Cloth, 30 cts.

Fior D'Aliza. By Alphonse de Lamartine, author of "Life of Mary Queen of Scotts," "History of the Girondists," etc. Translated from the French by George Perry. New edition, cloth, 25 cts.; half Russia, red edges, 30 cts.

Rip Van Winkle, and Other Sketches. By Washington Irving. Elzevir edition, 240 pages, Brevier type, leaded, printed on fine paper, with red border lines, and richly bound in extra cloth, gilt edges, black and gold ornaments. Price 35 cts.

LIBRARY OF POETRY.
All uniform, large 12mo., volumes.

Edwin Arnold, Brevier type, 414 pages, cloth, 50 cts.; gilt edges, ornamented, 70 cts.

Aytoun and Macaulay, Small Pica type, 446 Pages, cloth, 50 cts.; gilt edges, ornamented, 70 cts.

Burns, Brevier type, 584 pages, cloth, 50 cts.; gilt edges, ornamented, 70 cts.

Mrs. Browning, Brevier type, 624 pages, cloth, 55 cts.; gilt edges, ornamented, 75 cts.

Byron, Nonpareil type, 560 pages, cloth, 50 cts.; gilt edges, ornamented, 70 cts.

Campbell, Brevier type, 386 pages, cloth, 40 cts.; gilt edges, ornamented, 60 cts.

Chaucer, Bourgeois type, 636 pages, cloth, 60 cts.; gilt edges, ornamented, 80 cts.

Coleridge, Bourgeois type, 668 pages, cloth, 60 cts.; gilt edges, ornamented, 80 cts.

Cowper, Bourgeois type, 650 pages, cloth, 60 cts.; gilt edges, ornamented, 80 cts.

Crabbe, Brevier type, 540 pages, cloth, 50 cts.; gilt edges, ornamented, 70 cts.

Dante, Bourgeois type, 462 pages, cloth, 50 cts.; gilt edges, ornamented, 70 cts.

Dryden, Small Pica type, 444 pages, cloth, 50 cts.; gilt edges, ornamented, 70 cts.

George Eliot, Long Primer type, 356 pages, cloth, 40 cts.; gilt edges, ornamented, 60 cts.

Favorite Poems, Long Primer type, 454 pages, cloth, 45 cts.; gilt edges, ornamented, 65 cts.

Goethe, including Faust, Long Primer type, 836 pages, cloth, 70 cts.; gilt edges, ornamented, 90 cts.

Goldsmith, Long Primer type, 552 pages, cloth, 50 cts.; gilt edges, ornamented, 70 cts.

Hemans, Brevier type, 556 pages, cloth, 50 cts.; gilt edges, ornamented, 70 cts.

Herbert, Small Pica type, 594 pages, cloth, 50 cts.; gilt edges, ornamented, 70 cts.

Homer's Iliad and Odyssey, Bourgeois type, 835 pages, cloth, 70 cts.; gilt edges, ornamented, 90 cts.

Hood, Long Primer type, 602 pages, cloth, 50 cts.; gilt edges, ornamented, 70 cts.

Ingelow, Bourgeois type, 522 pages, cloth, 50 cts.; gilt edges, ornamented, 70 cts.

Keats, Small Pica type, 416 pages, cloth, 40 cts.; gilt edges, ornamented, 60 cts.

Meredith, including Lucile, Brevier type, 478 pages, cloth, 50 cts.; gilt edges, ornamented, 70 cts.

Milton, Long Primer type, 560 pages, cloth, 50 cts.; gilt edges, ornamented, 70 cts.

Moore, Brevier type, 670 pages, cloth, 60 cts.; gilt edges, ornamented, 80 cts.

Ossian, Long Primer type, 492 pages, cloth, 50 cts.; gilt edges, ornamented, 70 cts.

Poe, Pica type, 196 pages, cloth, 40 cts.; gilt edges, ornamented, 60 cts.

Poetry of Flowers, Long Primer type, 564 pages, cloth, 50 cts.; gilt edges, ornamented, 70 cts.

Pope, Long Primer type, 548 pages, cloth, 50 cts.; gilt edges, ornamented, 70 cts.

Proctor, Small Pica type, 444 pages, cloth, 45 cts.; gilt edges, ornamented, 65 cts.

Rogers, Pica type, 348 pages, cloth, 40 cts.; gilt edges, ornamented, 60 cts.

D. G. Rossetti, Long Primer type, 306 pages, cloth, 50 cts.; gilt edges, ornamented, 70 cts.

Schiller, Long Primer type, 350 pages, cloth, 40 cts.; gilt edges, ornamented, 60 cts.

Scott, Minion type, 666 pages, cloth, 50 cts.; gilt edges, ornamented, 70 cts.

Shakespeare, Nonpareil type, 1106 pages, cloth, 75 cts.; gilt edges, ornamented, 95 cts.

Shelley, Minion type, 578 pages, cloth, 50 cts.; gilt edges, ornamented, 70 cts.

Spenser, Nonpareil type, 714 pages, cloth, 70 cts.; gilt edges, ornamented, 90 cts.

H. Taylor, Long Primer type, 456 pages, cloth, 40 cts.; gilt edges, ornamented, 60 cts.

Tennyson, Brevier type, 730 pages, cloth, 60 cts.; gilt edges, ornamented, 80 cts.

Thomson, Small Pica type, 480 pages, cloth, 45 cts.; gilt edges, ornamented, 65 cts.

Virgil, Brevier type, 426 pages, cloth, 45 cts.; gilt edges, ornamented, 65 cts.

Charles Wesley, Long Primer type, 398 pages,
cloth, 45 cts.; gilt edges, ornamented 65 cts.

H. Kirke White, Bourgeois type, 490 pages, cloth,
50 cts.; gilt edges, ornamented, 70 cts.

N. P. Willis, Small Pica type, 324 pages, cloth,
40 cts.; gilt edges, ornamented, 60 cts.

Wordsworth, Minion type, 710 pages, cloth, 60
cts.; gilt edges, ornamented, 80 cts.

Poetical Concordance, Bourgeois type, cloth, $1;
gilt edges, ornamented, $1.20.

SELECT POEMS.

The Light of Asia. By Edwin Arnold. With a
life of the author, and very full and valuable notes, by Mrs.
I. L. Hauser. 16mo., 240 pages, Small Pica type, leaded.
Cloth, 25 cts.

Pearls of the Faith: or, Islam's Rosary. By Edwin
Arnold. Elzevir edition, 202 pages, Brevier type, leaded. Cloth,
25 cts.

The Indian Song of Songs: a Sanscrit Idyl. By
Edwin Arnold. Elzevir edition, 71 pages, Brevier type, leaded.
Cloth, 25 cts.

Studies in Stanzas, Tints of the Times, Ballads
and Broadsides. By Orpheus C. Kerr. 228 pages, Pica type,
leaded. Cloth, gilt edges, ornamented, 35 cts.

Hamlet. By Shakespeare. Elzevir edition, 144
pages, Brevier type, leaded. Cloth, 20 cts.

SCIENCE.

Insects at Home: Being a popular account of all
those insects which are useful or destructive. Illustrated
with engravings of upwards of 700 figures. By J. G. Wood,
M.A., F.L.S., author of "Homes without Hands;" "Bible
Animals;" "Common Objects of the Sea-shore and Country;"
"Illustrated Natural History;" "Strange Dwellings," etc.
690 pages, large octavo, Small Pica type, leaded. Half Russia,
red edges, $1.50.

Library of Science, Vol. 1. Model Octavo, 657
pages, Long Primer type, and Brevier, 74 illustrations. Half
Russia, red edges, $1.50. Contains :

Origin of Nations. Geo. Rawlinson.
Evolutionist at Large. Grant Allen.
Landholding in England. J. Fisher.
Fashion in Deformity. W. H. Flower.
Facts and Fictions in Zoology. A. Wilson.
The Study of Words. R. C. Trench.
Hereditary Traits, etc. R. A. Proctor.
Vignettes from Nature. Grant Allen.
Philosophy of Style. Herbert Spencer.
The Mother Tongue. Alex. Bain.
Religions of India. John Caird.
Religion of China. Geo. Matheson.
Religion of Persia. John Milne.
Evolution and Biology. T. H. Huxley.

NEW PRICE LIST.—*Continued.*

Library of Science Vol. II. Model Octavo, 778 pages. Bourgeois type, 105 illustrations. Half Russia, $1.50. Contents:

Light Science for Leisure Hours. R. A. Proctor.
The Forms of Water. J. Tyndall.
Physics and Politics. W. Bagehot.
Man's Place in Nature. T. H. Huxley.
Education. Herbert Spencer.
Town Geology. Chas. Kingsley.
Conservation of Energy. Balfour Stewart.
Study of Languages. C. Marcel.
Data of Ethics. Herbert Spencer.
Sound in Relation to Music. Blaserna.
Naturalists on the Amazon. Bates.

Library of Science, Vol. III. Model Octavo edition, 652 pages, Bourgeois type, 121 illustrations. Half Russia, $1.50. Contains:

Mind and Body. Alex. Bain.
Wonders of the Heavens. Flammarion.
Longevity. John Gardner.
Origin of Species. T. H. Huxley.
Progress: Its Law and Cause. Spencer.
Lessons in Electricity. Tyndall.
Familiar Essays. R. A. Proctor.
Romance of Astronomy. R. K. Miller.
Physical Basis of Life. T. H. Huxley.
Seeing and Thinking. W. K. Clifford.
Scientific Sophisms. Wainwright.
Popular Scientific Lectures. Helmholtz.

Library of Science, Vol. IV. Model Octavo, 600 pages. Long Primer type, and Brevier, with 47 illustrations. Half Russia, red edges, $1.50. Contains:

Lectures on Light. J. Tyndall.
Geological Sketches. Geikie.
Scientific evidences of Organic Evolution. Geo. Romanes.
Palaeontology and Evolution. T. H. Huxley.
Natural Selection and Natural Theology. Eustace R. Conder.
Current Discussions in Science. W. M. Williams.
Science in Politics. Frederick Pollock.
Darwin and Humboldt. Huxley, Romanes, Geikie, Dyer, and Prof. Agassiz.
Dawn of History. C. F. Keary.
Diseases of Memory. Th. Ribot.
Childhood of Religions. Edward Clodd.
Life in Nature. James Hinton.

Health by Exercise. By George H. Taylor, M.D. Large 12mo., Long Primer type, 408 pages, with numerous illustrations. Cloth, 45 cts.

Health for Women. By George H. Taylor, M.D. New Elzevir edition, 249 pages, Brevier type, leaded. Cloth, 30 cts.

The Nerves: Paralysis and other Affections of the nerves; their cure, by transmitted energy and special movements. By Geo. H. Taylor, M.D. Large 12mo., Pica type, 173 pages. Cloth, 40 cts.　　　11

www.ingramcontent.com/pod-product-compliance
Lightning Source LLC
Chambersburg PA
CBHW030717110426
42739CB00030B/708